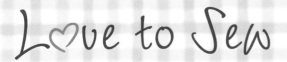

Love to Sew

Zakka-Style Gifts

Cecilia
Hanselmann

Search Press

First published in Great Britain 2014 by Search Press Limited
Wellwood, North Farm Road, Tunbridge Wells, Kent TN2 3DR

Reprinted 2014

Original German edition published as *Zakka-Style! Kleine Nähprojekte für einen bunten Alltag!*

Copyright © 2013 Christophorus Verlag GmbH, Freiburg/Germany

Text copyright © Cecilia Hanselmann 2013

English translation by Burravoe Translation Services

ISBN: 978-1-78221-059-7

Designs: Cecilia Hanselmann
Technical drawings: Claudia Schmidt
Photography: Uli Glasemann
Styling: Elke Reith

The publishers and author can accept no responsibility for any consequences arising from the information, advice or instructions given in this publication.

Printed in China

Glass Holder, page 14

Pot Holder, page 16

Coasters, page 22

Bottle Bag, page 24

Bookmark, page 34

Pencil Case, page 36

Camera Pouch, page 46

Handbag Organiser, page 48

Love to Sew

Zakka-Style Gifts

Contents

Apron, page 18

Tea Towel, page 20

Shopping Bag, page 26

Table Baskets, page 28

Place Mat, page 30

Book Cover, page 32

Owl Paperweight, page 38

Pin Cushion, page 40

Sakura Box Bag, page 42

Mini Wallet, page 44

Tissue Holder, page 50

Key Purse, page 52

Coin Purse, page 54

Shoulder Bag, page 56

Introduction

You may well be asking yourself 'what exactly is Zakka?' The word Zakka originates from a Japanese word which originally meant 'household items'. However, in recent years it has increasingly been used to mean homemade everyday items.

In this book, I shall be showing you a wide range of pretty little accessories, all lovingly hand-made, that will add a touch of colour to your daily life. It's not just the brightly coloured fabrics that make these items so special, there are also simple yet effective patchworking and quilt-as-you-go techniques to make these designs even more impressive.

The quilt-as-you-go technique involves partly quilting and lining the fabric while you sew. The patchwork technique will help make use of all the treasured fabric pieces from your remnants box and turn them into miniature works of art. Both techniques are described in detail with illustrated step-by-step guides at the front of the book.

Every single project you make will be unique, memorable, and will have plenty of character.

I hope you enjoy making them!

With best wishes,

Cecilia Hanselmann

Sewing basics

Please read this section before you begin the projects because it contains useful information to help you achieve the best results.

Ironing

Always iron the fabric before you start to sew and after completing each stage of your work. Take extra care with synthetic or delicate fabrics; cover them with a clean cotton cloth when ironing to be on the safe side.
NB: To avoid constant repetition throughout the book, instructions for ironing are not always provided.

Tension

Adjust the tension on your sewing machine to suit the particular fabric, otherwise you could end up with loops in the upper or lower thread. Ideally, always try out the stitching on a test piece first.

Straight stitch

This is the basic utility stitch on a sewing machine. It might also be called lockstitch. You can adjust the stitch length to suit your purposes. The longer the stitch, the looser the seam will be.

Tacking and pinning

Before sewing, always secure the pieces of fabric by tacking the seams by hand or pinning them. This will prevent the pieces of fabric from sliding and creases from forming when you sew them together.

The fabric grain

Every material is made up of warp threads (lengthways) and weft threads (crossways). The fabric grain corresponds to the direction of the warp threads, and goes parallel to the selvedge. The fabric should always be cut along the grain to prevent the sewn item from distorting.

Seam allowance

The seam may easily pull apart if a fabric is sewn too close to the edge. A seam allowance of 0.75cm (¼in) is generally used in this book, but if you are a beginner you may wish to add a larger seam allowance of 1cm (½in) or even 1.5cm (⅝in) and then trim it back after stitching. The width of the seam allowance is given under 'Cutting out' in the instructions.

Right and wrong side of the fabric

Every piece of fabric has a right and a wrong side. The right side is the side that we see on the finished project, i.e. the outside of the fabric. This is easy to identify on printed fabrics, as it is the side clearly displaying the pattern. So when the instructions tell you to 'place the pieces of fabric with the right sides facing', this means that the right sides should be together on the inside, and the wrong sides (the sides we don't normally see) are on the outside. Conversely, if the instructions say 'wrong sides facing', then the right sides should be on the outside, so that the wrong sides face each other on the inside.

Patterns and templates

Most of the designs are made from simple rectangles or squares of fabric, and their dimensions are given in the instructions under 'Cutting out'. Templates for some of the designs are included at the back of the book. I suggest you trace the templates on to tracing or similar paper beforehand. When instructed to in the project, be sure to transfer the markings as well.

Materials

- ♥ Sewing machine
- ♥ Matching thread (cotton)
- ♥ Sewing needles
- ♥ Pins
- ♥ Small sewing scissors
- ♥ Pattern paper, pencil/pen
- ♥ Tailor's chalk
- ♥ Fabric (dressmaking) scissors
- ♥ Pinking shears
- ♥ Rotary cutter
- ♥ Seam ripper
- ♥ Tape measure
- ♥ Iron
- ♥ Cutting mat
- ♥ Patchwork ruler
- ♥ Fabric marker

Note: The items given in the materials list above are the basic items you will need for all projects and to avoid repetition they will not be listed in the individual project instructions.

Cutting on the fold

Some of the patterns in this book should be cut from folded fabric. Place the pattern piece on the folded fabric with the broken line marked on the pattern directly over the fold. Cut through both fabric layers at once.

Zigzag stitch

Zigzag stitch is an extremely useful stitch on a sewing machine. It is used to neaten the fabric edges. The stitch length and width can be adjusted. A very tight zigzag stitch can also be used to attach fabric and prevent fraying without needing to fold down the edges.

Cutting out

Cutting the fabric out is just as important as the sewing process. First make a pattern on tracing or thin cardboard to the measurements provided or to the template. Pin this pattern to the wrong side of the fabric and draw around it with tailor's chalk or a fabric marker. Then add any seam allowances on all sides. Cut the item out with sharp fabric (dressmaking) scissors or a rotary cutter. Special circle cutters are suitable for cutting regular circles.

Sewing techniques

Securing stitching/seams

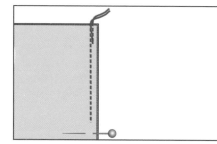

You must secure the beginning and end of a machine-sewn seam, otherwise it will unravel. At the beginning of the seam, sew three or four stitches forwards, then back, and then forwards again. Do the same at the end of the seam.

Snipping into seam allowances

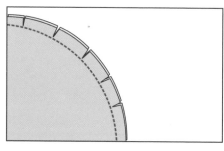

For rounded items, make a series of cuts, at small intervals, approximately 1mm from the stitching. Turn the item right sides out. The cuts will ensure that the edge is nice and flat when the fabric is right sides out because the additional width of the seam allowance is more neatly distributed.

Overedge stitch

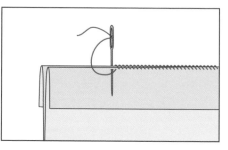

This hand stitch is used to close a turning hole. Push the sewing needle vertically through the fabric edges very close to the edge. The very small stitches are linked by sloping threads. Secure the beginning and end well.

Inserting a zip

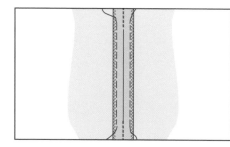

1 Press the seam allowances back along the seam where the zip will be placed. You may find it helpful to tack the seam allowances in place.

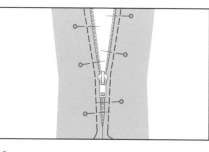

2 Attach the zip foot to the sewing machine. Turn the item right sides out and tack or pin the zip under the opening as shown. Sew one side of the zip 0.5cm (¼in) from the fold.

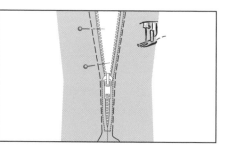

3 Leave the needle down in the fabric when you get to the bottom of the zip. Raise the zipper foot, turn the item, and sew at a right angle from the first side over to the second side. Leave the needle in the fabric as before, then raise the zipper foot and turn the item again. Then sew the second side.

Creating neat corners and curves

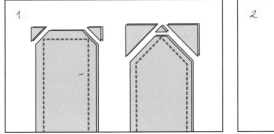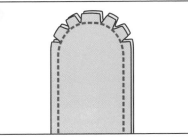

Crisp corners and smooth curves are the hallmarks of well-sewn items. Cut your pieces carefully and sew using the width of your sewing-machine foot as a guide unless otherwise stated. Pivot the fabric with the needle in the down position at corners and regular intervals on curves. For best results, on corners and angles trim the seam allowances at intervals as shown in 2.

Shaping bag bases

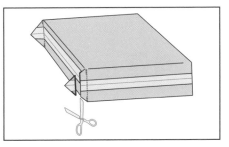

To shape the base of a bag, fold the side seams against the bottom edge on each side, aligning the seams, and sew a triangle in the stated width as shown. Trim the triangles back to the width of the seam allowance and neaten.

Preparing strips for handles

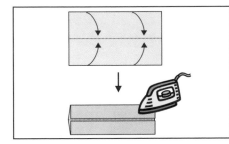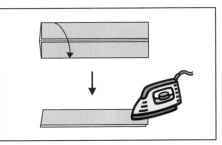

1 Fold the strip in half lengthways and iron lightly down the fold. Open the strip out again, then fold the two long sides from the outside so that they meet at the middle fold and iron.

2 Fold the strip in half again along the first fold line, as shown above, and iron well.

Appliqué

Transfer the motifs on to fusible webbing (e.g. Bondaweb), cut out, then iron on to the back of the appliqué fabric and cut out carefully. Remove the paper backing, iron on to the right side of the background fabric, and sew the edges.

Patchworking

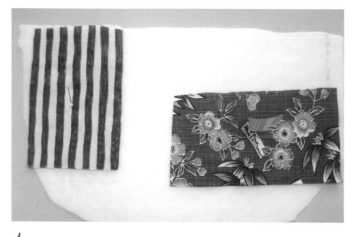

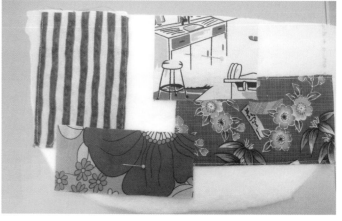

1 Cut out the fleece batting in the basic shape that you want with a generous seam allowance, and place the fabric remnants on top of it, overlapping slightly. You can also cut the 'patches' out with pinking shears or tear them.

2 Arrange the fabric pieces together until you have achieved the right balance. Now secure each piece with a pin in the middle so that you can stitch the edges.

3 Using a sewing machine, edgestitch each piece of fabric in place using straight stitches, starting with the bottom pieces first. To edgestitch, simply stitch just inside the fabric edge.

4 You can experiment with different stitch lengths and styles as you work. Remember that precision is not all that important with this technique.

Quilt-as-you-go

1 Place the lining fabric right side down and place the volume fleece batting on top. Position the first patchwork strip on top of it right side up.

2 Place the second patchwork strip, right sides facing and right-hand edges matching, on to the first one and sew through all the layers with a foot-width's seam allowance.

3 Fold the second strip over so the right side is showing and iron the seam in place.

4 Repeat steps 2 and 3 until you have sewn all the strips together as desired to create a large-enough piece.

5 This is what the item looks like when it has not yet been trimmed to the required size.

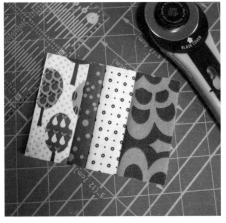

6 Trim the item to the desired dimensions, ideally using a patchwork ruler and a rotary cutter on a cutting mat.

Glass Holder

Size: for 1 glass, approximately 7.5cm (3in) in diameter

Materials

For the outside and lining:
- ♥ 5 pieces of printed cotton fabric 6.5 x 10cm (2½ x 4in)
- ♥ 6.5 x 9cm (2½ x 3½in) of printed cotton fabric for the flap
- ♥ 12 x 30cm (4¾ x 12in) of printed cotton fabric for the lining

For the padding:
- ♥ 12 x 30cm (4¾ x 12in) of insulating volume fleece batting

Additional pieces:
- ♥ 4cm (1½in) of hook-and-loop fastener (e.g. Velcro)
- ♥ 75cm (30in) of bias binding in a matching colour

Sewing

1 Place the lining fabric wrong side up and position the volume fleece batting on top. Sew the fabric strips on using the quilt-as-you-go technique (see page 13). Trim the piece to 8 x 24cm (3¼ x 9½in).

2 Attach bias binding on all sides. To do this see the section below.

3 For the flap, place the fabric right side up and fold widthways with right sides facing; sew the sides together, leaving a turning hole. Turn the right way out, then iron and sew up the turning hole by hand.

Finishing off

1 Sew the soft side of the hook-and-loop fastener to one longer edge of the flap.

2 Sew the flap on to one end of the quilted item so that there is a 2cm (¾in) overlap at the edge with the hook-and-loop fastener attached.

3 Sew the rough piece of the hook-and-loop fastener on to the opposite end of the quilted piece.

Attach binding

1 Unfold the bias binding and turn the end to the wrong side by about 1cm (½in).

2 Pin the binding to the fabric with the right sides facing, raw edges matching and with the turned end partway along one edge of the quilted piece. Stitch along the first fold line of the binding. Mitre the binding at the corners. When you get about 5cm (2in) from the starting point, stop and trim the end of the binding so that it overlaps the start by about 1.5cm (⅝in). Continue stitching to the end.

3 Fold the binding over to the wrong side of the quilted piece and pin in place with the long binding edge folded under. For the neatest results, hand stitch this in place with the long binding edge folded under. Alternatively you can stitch it in place by machine.

Pot Holder

Materials

For one pot holder:
- ♥ 6 different printed cotton fabric scraps each 30cm (12in) long with various widths of 3.5–6cm (1½–2½in)
- ♥ 30 x 30cm (12 x 12in) of printed cotton fabric for the backing

For the padding:
- ♥ 30 x 30cm (12 x 12in) of insulating volume fleece batting

Additional requirements:
- ♥ 14mm (½in) eyelet ring and fitting tool
- ♥ 110cm (43in) of bias binding in a matching colour

Size: 22 x 22cm (8¾ x 8¾in) for one pot holder

Sewing

1 Neaten the edges of your fabric scraps so that they are fairly straight and not frayed.

2 Place the backing fabric wrong side up and position the volume fleece batting on top.

3 Sew the fabric strips on using the quilt-as-you-go technique (see page 13). Trim the piece to 22 x 22cm (8¾ x 8¾in).

4 Attach bias binding on all sides (see page 14).

Finishing off

Insert the eyelet ring into one corner of the pot holder following the manufacturer's instructions. If you wish, make a second pot holder in the same way.

Apron

Materials

For the outside and lining:
- 60 x 110cm (24 x 43in) of natural-coloured linen for the apron
- 45 x 110cm (18 x 43in) of printed cotton fabric for the pockets and ties

Cutting out

Dimensions include 0.75cm (¼in) seam allowance.
- Cut two pieces of natural-coloured linen 47 x 54cm (18½ x 21½in) for the front and lining of the apron
- Cut two pieces of printed cotton fabric 9.5 x 80.5cm (3¾ x 31¾in) (for the ties)
- Cut two pieces of printed cotton fabric 30 x 15cm (12 x 6in) (for the pockets)

Preparation

Use the scallop template on page 59 to mark out and cut the bottom edge of the linen fabric.

Size: 45 x 52cm (17¾ x 20½in) (plus ties)
Template: see page 59

Sewing

1 For the ties, fold each of the fabric strips in half lengthways, right sides facing, and stitch along the long side and one end. Turn the right way out. Position the ties lying horizontally along the top of one of the linen pieces, one seam allowance from the top edge, with the stitched ends pointing towards the centre.

2 Pin then stitch the two linen pieces together with right sides facing. Sew the bottom scalloped edge according to the template and leave a turning hole at one side. Trim the seam allowance on the scalloping, snipping up to the stitching at the points but being careful not to cut the stitching. Turn the right way out, then iron and sew up the turning hole by hand (see page 10).

3 Fold the pockets in half widthways with right sides facing and sew together, leaving a turning hole. Turn the right way out, then iron and sew up the turning hole by hand (see page 10).

Finishing off

Place the pockets on the apron 11cm (4½in) from the top and 8cm (3¼in) in from each side edge. Edgestitch the sides and bottom, stitching close to the edge of the fabric. Reinforce the stitching at the top edge by working back and forth over a few stitches.

Tip

Buy extra linen so you can make the Tea Towel on page 20 as well.

Tea Towel

Materials

- 50 x 110cm (20 x 43in)
  of natural-coloured linen
- 8 x 20cm (3¼ x 8in) of printed cotton
  fabric for the hanging loops
- 38 different remnants of printed cotton
  fabric measuring 8 x 8cm (3¼ x 3¼in)

Cutting out

Dimensions include 0.75cm (¼in) seam
allowance.

- Cut one piece of linen fabric
  46.5 x 61.5cm (18½ x 24¼in) for
  the tea towel
- Cut 38 pieces of fabric 6.5 x 6.5cm
  (2½ x 2½in) for the border
- Cut one piece of printed cotton 6 x 17cm
  (2½ x 6¾in) for the hanging loop

Sewing

1 Make the hanging loop as described on page 11 for the handle.

2 Fold the loop and place it in the middle of the top of the tea towel with the loop pointing upwards from the towel.

3 To make the top and bottom borders, make two strips each of seven small squares, joining each square side by side (include a seam allowance of 0.75cm (¼in) for each square). For the right and left borders of the tea towel, make two strips of twelve small squares in the same way as before. Iron all the seams open and then fold in and press one long edge of each strip by 0.75cm (¼in) to the wrong side.

4 Take the shorter strips and sew the unironed long edges to the top and bottom edges of the tea towel, right sides of the strips facing the wrong side of the tea towel fabric. Now fold the strips over to the right side of the tea towel and edgestitch them in place along the fold line. Do the same with the longer strips to make the sides of the tea towel.

Finishing off

Edgestitch around all four edges of the tea towel.

Materials

For one coaster:
- 6 different remnants of large-print cotton fabric approximately 1–6cm (½–2½in) wide and 4–13cm (1¾–5¼in) long
- 15 x 15cm (6 x 6in) of printed cotton fabric for the backing

For the padding:
- 15 x 15cm (6 x 6in) of thin volume fleece batting

Coasters

Size: 11 x 11cm (4½ x 4½in)

Sewing

1 Arrange the fabric remnants on the volume fleece batting, pin in place and then sew each one on using a zigzag stitch (see page 9) with matching or coordinating thread.

2 Trim the patchwork piece to 11 x 11cm (4½ x 4½in).

Finishing off

Place the 15 x 15cm (6 x 6in) square of backing fabric and the patchwork piece wrong sides together, and sew the edges together using a zigzag stitch. Make other coasters in the same way.

Materials

For the outside and lining:
- 110 x 30cm (43 x 12in) of spotted green cotton fabric
- 4 different coloured fabric remnants 6 x 30cm (2½ x 12in)

For the padding:
- 25 x 35cm (10 x 13¾in) of volume fleece batting
- 1 piece using the base template of volume fleece batting

Additional requirements:
- 50cm (20in) cord

Cutting out

Dimensions include 0.75cm (¼in) seam allowance. When cutting out to the template, add 0.75cm (¼in) on all sides.

In spotted green fabric:
- Cut one piece 14 x 27.5cm (5½ x 10¾in) for the drawstring section
- Cut two pieces using the templates for the base and the lining for the base
- Cut one piece 25 x 35cm (10 x 13¾in) for the bag lining
- Cut one piece of 6 x 38cm (2½ x 15in) for the strap

Bottle Bag

Size: 8cm (3¼in) diameter, 24cm (9½in) tall
Template: page 58

Sewing

1 Lay out the 25 x 35cm (10 x 13¾in) rectangle of green spotted fabric for the lining, wrong side up, and place the matching volume fleece batting on top. Using the quilt-as-you-go technique (see page 13), sew the four fabric strips on top. Trim the patchwork piece to 19.5 x 27.5cm (7¾ x 10¾in) and zigzag around all the edges to secure them. Fold the piece in half, widthways, with right sides facing and matching the short edges together. Stitch this seam, forming a tube with the fabric.

2 To prepare the base, place the volume fleece batting on the wrong side of the base fabric. Then place the base lining, right side up, on top of the fleece. Sew around in zigzag stitch to secure.

3 Sew the base into the tube of fabric along the lining edge, making sure to get the spacing right to prevent wrinkles.

4 For the strap, fold the rectangle as directed on page 11 then edgestitch the long edges. Tack the strap ends to the top of the patchwork cylinder, with one end on each side.

5 For the drawstring section at the top of the bag, fold the 14 x 27.5cm (5½ x 10¾in) rectangle in half with right sides facing and short edges matching. Stitch the 14cm (10¾in) seam, leaving a 2cm (¾in) gap in the centre and securing the stitching firmly on either side of the gap. Open out your fabric tube and press the seam allowances open. Fold the tube in half the other way, right sides out, so that the 27.5cm (10¾in) edges match. Zigzag stitch the raw edges together to secure the layers. Make the casing by stitching 1cm (⅜in) from the folded edge. The cord will be inserted through the small gap you left earlier.

6 Turn the casing section upside down and slip it over the patchwork bottle bag, which should be right sides out. Match the raw edges of both sections. The ends of the strap should be caught between the layers. Stitch around the top of the bag. Fold up the casing section and press if needed.

Finishing off

Thread the cord through the hole in the seam at the top of the bottle bag and around the casing, pulling it out at the other end. Knot the ends of the cord together.

Materials

For the outside:
- ♥ 140 x 60cm (43 x 24in)
  of natural-coloured linen
- ♥ 3 printed or plain print cotton
  fabric pieces at least:
  15 x 15cm (6 x 6in) in red
  20 x 13cm (8 x 5in) in yellow
  7 x 15cm (2¾ x 6in) in green

For the appliqué:
- ♥ 20 x 45cm (8 x 18in) of fusible webbing
  (e.g. Bondaweb)

Cutting out

Dimensions include 0.75cm (¼in)
seam allowance.
- ♥ Cut two pieces of natural-coloured linen
  38.5 x 48.5cm (15 x 19in) for the bag
- ♥ Cut two pieces of natural-coloured linen
  46 x 14cm (18 x 5½in) for the handles

Shopping Bag

Size: 37 x 47cm (14½ x 18½in) (plus handles)
Templates: page 58

Sewing

1 To make the handles, fold the linen strips in half lengthways and iron. Open out, fold the long side edges towards the middle fold and iron (taking care not to iron out the middle fold). Iron the seam allowances on the short ends to the inside. Fold each strip in half lengthways along the first fold and iron. Edgestitch along both sides.

2 Iron the fusible webbing on to the wrong side of all the coloured fabrics. Using the templates on page 58, carefully cut out the motifs from the coloured fleeced fabrics. Arrange the motifs on the outside of one of the linen rectangles and iron to fuse in place. Sew along the edges of the motifs in a tight zigzag (stitch length 0.5mm, stitch width 2mm).

3 Place the pieces for the bag together with the right sides facing. Sew the sides and bottom together, and finish off. Sew the base corners at a width of 10cm (4in) as described on page 11.

4 Fold in the top edges by 3cm (1¼in) and iron. Fold under the raw edge on the inside of the bag and edgestitch.

Finishing off

Position the ends of the handles on the top edge of the bag, 9cm (3½in) from the side edges and overlapping by 3cm (1¼in). Edgestitch the ends neatly into place on the top edge of the bag to finish.

Table Baskets

Materials

For one square and one rectangular basket:
- 20 x 20cm (8 x 8in) of printed cotton fabric (square basket)
- 40 x 22cm (15¾ x 8¾in) of printed cotton fabric (rectangular basket)
- 20 x 20cm (8 x 8in) of natural-coloured linen (square basket)
- 40 x 22cm (15¾ x 8¾in) of natural-coloured linen (rectangular basket)

For stiffening:
- 20 x 90cm (8 x 35½in) of medium firm iron-on interfacing (square basket)
- 25 x 90cm (10 x 35½in) of medium firm iron-on interfacing (rectangular basket)

Additional requirements:
- Water-erasable fabric marker pen

Cutting out

When cutting to templates A and B, add 0.75cm (¼in) seam allowance on all sides.
- Cut one piece each from templates A and B in printed cotton fabric for the inner pieces
- Cut one piece each from templates A and B in natural-coloured linen for the outer pieces
- Cut two pieces each from templates A and B of interfacing for stiffening

Size: 10 x 10cm (4 x 4in) and 9.5 x 26cm (3¾ x 10¼in)
Templates A and B: pages 59 and 60

Sewing

1 For both baskets, iron the interfacing on to the back of both pieces of linen.

2 Place the printed cotton fabric and the linen together with right sides facing and sew together on all sides, leaving a turning hole.

3 Trim back the seam allowance and cut diagonally across the corners (see page 11). Turn right sides out and iron. Hand stitch the turning hole closed. Use the fabric pen to draw the lines as shown on the template. Sew along these lines to make the folds. Iron the sides (walls) to the middle along the folds.

Finishing off

Sew together the top corners of the sides with a few strong hand stitches.

Place Mat

Materials

For one place mat:
- 140 x 35cm (43 x 14in) of natural-coloured linen
- Approximately 9 different-sized remnants of print cotton fabric, e.g. 5 x 23cm (2 x 9in), 6 x 7cm (2½ x 2¾in), 2 x 7cm (¾ x 2¾in), etc.

For the padding:
- 35 x 45cm (12¾ x 17¾in) of lightweight iron-on volume fleece batting

Cutting out

Dimensions include 0.75cm (¼in) seam allowance.
- Cut two pieces of natural-coloured linen 31.5 x 41.5cm (12½ x 16¼in) for the front and back
- Trim the edges of the printed cotton fabric as desired, e.g. smooth or with pinking shears, or you can even tear them

Size: 30 x 40cm (12 x 16in)

Sewing

1 To make the front, iron volume fleece batting on to the wrong side of one linen rectangle. Arrange the trimmed fabric remnants on top of the linen and sew on using the patchwork technique (see page 12) with straight and zigzag stitching.

2 Place the remaining piece of linen on top with the right sides facing and sew together on all sides, leaving a turning hole in one edge.

Finishing off

Turn the place mat right sides out, then iron and hand sew the turning hole closed. Make other place mats in the same way.

Tip

Use insulating volume fleece batting instead of standard fleece in your mats to help protect your table from heat damage.

Book Cover

Size: 12 x 19cm (4¾ x 7½in) (to fit one average sized book)

Materials

For the outside and lining:
- 70 x 25cm (27½ x 10in) of red and white spotted cotton fabric
- 70 x 25cm (27½ x 10in) of large-print pattern cotton fabric

Cutting out

Dimensions include 0.75cm (¼in) seam allowance.

- Cut one piece of red and white spotted fabric 17.5 x 21cm (7 x 8¼in) for the book spine and one piece 41.5 x 21cm (16½ x 8¼in) for the lining
- Cut two pieces of large-print pattern fabric 13.5 x 21cm (5¼ x 8¼in) for the front and back

Sewing

1 With right sides facing, sew a large-print pattern rectangle to each end of the red and white spotted rectangle piece for the book spine along the 21cm (8¼in) edges. Press the seams open and iron.

2 Pin this piece to the red and white spotted lining piece with right sides facing and stitch together all round, leaving a turning hole of about 6cm (2½in).

3 Turn the right way, then iron and sew up the turning hole by hand (see page 10).

Finishing off

Fold the short sides over to the lining by 3cm (1¼in) each side, then press and edgestitch the top and bottom edges.

Tip

Check to make sure the size is right for your favourite book and adjust appropriately. Depending on how thick it is, the ends might have to be folded over a little more or less.

Materials

For one bookmark:
- 20 x 30cm (8 x 12in) of natural-coloured linen
- 10 different-sized rectangular pieces of printed cotton fabric

Additional requirements:
- Corded ribbon: 30cm (12in)

Cutting out

- Cut one piece of natural-coloured linen 23 x 8cm (9 x 3¼in) for the base
- Cut one piece of natural-coloured linen 19 x 8cm (7½ x 3¼in) for the back

Bookmark

Size: 5 x 19cm (2 x 7½in) plus the ribbon loop

Sewing

1 Arrange the printed cotton fabric remnants however you wish on the linen base and edgestitch into place using the patchwork technique (see page 12). Trim the finished patchwork piece to 5 x 19cm (2 x 7½in).

2 Place the back and patchwork pieces together, wrong sides facing, and pin. Fold the corded ribbon in half and insert approximately 2cm (¾in) between the two layers at the top.

Finishing off

Edgestitch around all four edges of the bookmark. You can use a straight stitch, as shown, or a zigzag stitch if you want to reduce fraying.

déguster jardiner au fil des saisons...

VOICI UN LIV

dans un jardin

Tu peux aussi

Une page à la fin

marquer les évén

dans le calendrier des pages suivantes.

le butiner et t'y promener, comme

admirer une fleur ou un fruit

c lui tes premiers pas de jard

de prendre des notes et tu

ants de ta vie de jardinier (semis, récol

Materials

For the outside and lining:
- 140 x 20cm (43 x 8in) of natural-coloured linen
- 15 x 16cm (6 x 6¼in) of printed cotton mushroom-motif fabric

For the padding:
- 25 x 30cm (10 x 12in) of thin iron-on volume fleece batting

Additional requirements:
- 1 zip: 20cm (8in)
- 15 x 15cm (6 x 6in) of fusible webbing

Cutting out

Dimensions include 0.75cm (¼in) seam allowance.
- Cut two pieces of natural-coloured linen 14.5 x 21.5cm (5¾ x 8½in) and two pieces of natural-coloured linen 7.5 x 21.5cm (3 x 8½in) for the case
- Cut one piece of mushroom printed cotton 4 x 16cm (1½ x 6¼in) for the loop
- Cut one piece of volume fleece batting 14.5 x 21.5cm (5½ x 8½in) and one piece 7.5 x 21.5cm (3 x 8½in)

Tip

If you don't have any mushroom-motif fabric, cut mushroom shapes from any fabric using the templates on page 60.

Pencil Case

Size: 10 x 20cm (4 x 8in)
Templates: page 60 (optional)

Sewing

1 Iron each fleece rectangle on to the back of a corresponding linen rectangle.

2 Iron the fusible webbing on to the back of the mushroom-motif fabric and carefully cut out three mushrooms (or use the templates to cut your mushrooms). Peel off the backing paper and position the motifs on the right side of the small fleeced linen rectangle. Iron to fuse into place then edgestitch around the mushrooms.

3 Tack the zip to the top long edge of the appliqué piece, right sides facing. Place the second (matching) linen rectangle on top, right side down, and stitch the zip edge in place. Flip the top layer of linen over to the back, press and then edgestitch close to the zip on the right side. Use the zip foot on your sewing machine.

4 Attach the other side of the zip to the larger linen rectangles in the same way and machine sew as before.

5 Sew the outside and lining together using zigzag stitch. They are treated as one piece in the following steps.

6 Make the loop as described on page 11 and sew on to the end of the zip; the loop should be on the zip and pointing to the inside.

7 Half open the zip and sew the base edges together, right sides facing.

8 Now sew the sides together, working from the corners of the bottom. Make sure that the zip is not on the fold, but approximately 3cm (1¼in) below the top edge.

Finishing off

Turn the pencil case right sides out and iron carefully.

Owl Paperweight

Size: 12cm (4¾in) high
Templates A–D: page 61

Materials

For the outside and lining:
- 30 x 40cm (12 x 15¾in) of printed cotton fabric for the body
- 30 x 20cm (12 x 8in) of printed cotton fabric for the tummy
- Scraps of black and brown craft felt for the eyes

Additional requirements:
- Toy stuffing
- Weights (e.g. old metal items such as screws, nuts and/or spacers)
- Brown embroidery thread
- Textile adhesive

Preparation

Cut out a pattern for the body and tummy to templates A and B, and for the eyes to templates C and D. The templates do not include a seam allowance.

Cutting out

Dimensions include 0.75cm (¼in) seam allowance. When cutting out to templates A and B, add 0.75cm (¼in) seam allowance on all sides.
- Cut one piece of cotton fabric of template A for the body
- Cut one piece of cotton fabric 6 x 6cm (2½ x 2½in) for the base
- Cut one piece of cotton fabric of template B for the tummy
- Cut two pieces of cotton fabric of template C in brown felt for the eyes
- Cut two pieces of template D in black felt for the pupils

Sewing

1 Sew the body and tummy together, right sides facing, along edges A and B, making sure that the seams meet exactly at the tip. Iron and turn right sides out. Sew two rows of running stitches along the bottom edge, which you will gather later on.

2 Stitch across the top edge of the body fabric piece diagonally 5cm (2in) from the tip to form the beak. Stuff the owl with toy filling and weights, making sure that the weights are on the inside and covered by the filling so they are not visible from the outside. Pull the gathering threads and knot the ends.

3 Iron the seam allowances on the base to the wrong side. Place the base over the gathered opening and stitch down by hand to close.

Finishing off

Pin the eyes to the sides of the beak, making sure they are roughly symmetrical, and then sew with embroidery thread using whip stitch. It is fine to let your stitches show as they add a hand-made look. Secure the pupils to the eyes with textile adhesive.

Pin Cushion

Size: 8 x 8cm (3¼ x 3¼in)

Materials

For one pin cushion:
- 10 x 10cm (4 x 4in) of printed cotton fabric
- 7 different pieces 3 x 15cm (1¼ x 6in) of printed cotton fabric

Additional requirements:
- 15 x 15cm (6 x 6in) of thin volume fleece batting
- 1 button
- Synthetic toy filling

Cutting out

Dimensions include 0.75cm (¼in) seam allowance.
- Cut one piece 9.5 x 9.5cm (3¾ x 3¾in) of printed cotton fabric (back)
- Cut the printed cotton fabric remnants in strips of various widths 2.5–4cm (1–1¾in)

Sewing

1 Sew the different fabric strips diagonally to the volume fleece batting using the quilt-as-you-go technique (page 13) and then trim the square to 9.5 x 9.5cm (3¾ x 3¾in) with the stripes running diagonally across the square.

2 Place the right side of the patchwork square on the right side of the square of cotton fabric and sew all around the edges, leaving a turning hole in one side of about 4cm (1½in). Turn right sides out, then iron and stuff with toy filling. Hand sew the turning hole closed.

Finishing off

Sew the button to the middle of the top side using a double thread or buttonhole yarn, and being sure to pierce through all the layers and pull them together tightly.

Tip

The 0.75cm (¼in) seam allowance is the width of a standard straight-stitch sewing-machine foot. If you only have a multipurpose foot on your machine it is probably wider. In this case, you can still use the width of the foot as your sewing guide because the front piece is cut to size after stitching and your piece will still be big enough.

Materials

- 110 x 40cm (43¼ x15¾in) of red and white spotted cotton fabric for the outside
- 10 x 10cm (4 x 4in) of floral cotton fabric for the appliqué
- 140 x 35cm (43 x13¾in) of natural-coloured linen for the lining

For the padding:
- 40 x 40cm (15¾ x 15¾in) lightweight fusible volume fleece batting

Additional requirements:
- 1 zip, 30cm (12in), in a matching colour
- 10 x 10cm (4 x 4in) of double-sided iron-on fusible webbing

Cutting out

Dimensions include a 0.75cm (¼in) seam allowance. When cutting out to template A, add 0.75cm (¼in) seam allowance on all sides.

- Cut two pieces of red and white spotted cotton fabric using template A
- Cut one piece of red and white spotted cotton fabric 8 x 22cm (3¼ x 8¾in) for the loop
- Cut one piece of floral fabric 10 x 10cm (4 x 4in)
- Cut two pieces of volume fleece batting using template A
- Cut two pieces of linen using template A

Sakura Box Bag

Size: 22 x 12 x 12cm (8¾ x 4¾ x 4¾in)
Templates A and B: page 62

Sewing

1 For the outside, iron volume fleece batting on to the backs of both cut-out pieces of red and white spotted cotton fabric.

2 Place the floral fabric piece on to the iron-on fusible webbing and iron together. Using template B, cut the cherry blossom motif out very carefully. Pull off the backing paper when done.

3 Place the flower-shaped piece on to one of the red and white spotted bag pieces and iron on. Sew along the edges using a tight zigzag stitch (stitch length 0.5mm, stitch width 2mm).

4 Position the zip along the top edge of the appliqué piece, right sides facing, then top with a linen bag piece, right side down. Secure and stitch together along the edge.

5 Fold the pieces over together with the wrong sides facing. Iron, then edgestitch along the zip seam. Repeat for the other side of the zip. Sew the outside and lining together using a zigzag stitch. They are treated as one piece from now on.

6 Make the strip for the loop as described on page 11 and sew on to the end of the zip seam (the loop should be on the zip and pointing to the inside). Half open the zip. Sew the base edges together, right sides facing. Close the side seams (a1 + a2), then the side seams (b1 + b2).

Finishing off

Turn the bag right sides out through the zip opening.

Mini Wallet

Size: 8 x 11.5cm (3¼ x 4½in)

Sewing

1 Place the volume fleece batting on the wrong side of the lining and sew the fabric strips on top using the quilt-as-you-go technique (see page 13). Trim the piece to 20.5 x 11.5cm (8 x 4½in).

2 Sew the bias binding to the short ends. Sew each half of the hook-and-loop fastener along the centre of each of the short ends 1cm (½in) from the corners, sewing the rough side on the inside edge and the soft side on to the outer flap.

3 Fold the bottom ends (outer side) 8cm (3¼in) to the left and iron. Sew bias binding to the unfinished edges.

Finishing off

Fold over the top end (flap) so that the two parts of the hook-and-loop fastener join. Press the wallet carefully.

Tip

When attaching the hook-and-loop fastener, use a bobbin thread that matches the patchwork, not the hook-and-loop fastener, so that it does not show on the right side of the wallet.

Materials

For one wallet:
- 25 x 15cm (10 x 6in) of printed cotton fabric
- 10 different printed cotton scraps, each 15cm (6in) long and in different widths (2.5–5cm; 1–2in)

For the padding:
- 25 x 15cm (10 x 6in) of thin volume fleece batting

Additional requirements:
- 7.5cm (3in) of hook-and-loop fastener (e.g. Velcro)
- 60cm (24in) of bias binding in a matching colour

Materials

For the outside and lining:
- 90 x 10cm (36 x 4in) of printed cotton fabric
- 15 x 70cm (6 x 10in) of natural-coloured linen

For the insert:
- 10 x 70cm (4 x 27½in) of thin fusible volume fleece batting

Cutting out

When cutting to the template do not add a seam allowance, but add 0.75cm (¼in) to the middle fold when cutting out the four fabric pieces for the outside.

- Cut four pieces of printed cotton fabric using the doubled version of the template (three outside pieces, one lining piece for the flap)
- Cut two pieces of linen using the doubled version of the template for the lining
- Cut one linen strip 4 x 70cm (1¾ x 27½in) for the strap
- Cut three pieces of volume fleece batting using the doubled version of the template

Tips

- To save time, use ribbon or braid instead of making your own bag straps.
- The wadding will stretch a little as you sew. Trim it back to the size of the cotton bag pieces as you go.

Camera Pouch

Size: 7.5 x 11cm (3 x 4½in)
Template: page 63

Sewing

1 Iron each piece of volume fleece batting on to the back of three cotton bag pieces. One cotton bag piece will not require fleece backing.

2 Pin two of the fleeced bag pieces together with right sides facing and stitch together around the curved edge, leaving the straight edge open and starting and stopping your stitching a seam's width from the straight edge. This is the main bag piece.

3 Repeat to stitch the fleeced and unfleeced cotton bag pieces together for the flap. Snip into the seam allowances on the curves of both joined pieces. Stitch the two linen pieces together for the lining, but this time leave a hole in the centre of the seam of about 4cm (1½in) at the bottom of the bag. Reinforce the stitching on each side of the hole.

4 Turn the flap right sides out and push out the curves. Trim the flap along the straight edge, if necessary, and then tack this edge together.

5 Make the strap by folding the linen strip as directed on page 11 and then edgestitch both long edges. Cut off a 6.5cm (2½in) length of the strap to make a small loop. The remaining length will create the large loop of the strap.

6 With the main bag section still inside out, fold down the seam allowance of the top layer and pin out of the way. Fold both lengths of strap in half and tack the ends of the smaller one to the centre top edge (not the pinned-back edge), matching the raw edges. Tack on the longer loop so the ends are either side of the smaller loop ends. Pin the flap centrally on top and stitch along the straight edge, joining the flap to the right side of the bag without catching the pinned-back edge in the stitching. The loops will be caught in the seam at the same time.

7 Unpin the pinned-back edge of the bag, turn the bag right sides out and fold the flap down so the straight edge at the top of the bag is exposed all round.

8 Slide the whole thing into the lining, right sides together and seams aligning. Stitch around the straight edge at the top of the bag.

Finishing off

Turn the bag out through and stitch the hole closed by hand.

Materials

Dimensions include a 0.75cm (¼in) seam allowance.

For the outside and lining:
You will need five different patterned cotton fabrics, labelled here A – E.
- 16.5 x 21.5cm (6½ x 8½in) of A for the outside
- 21.5 x 21.5cm (8½ x 8½in) of B for the large compartment
- 12.5 x 21.5cm (5 x 8½in) of B for the mobile compartment
- 7.5 x 22.5cm (3 x 9in) of C for the pen compartment
- 16.5 x 21.5cm (6½ x 8½in) of D for the outside
- Two pieces 16.5 x 21.5cm (6½ x 8½in) of E for the lining
- 15 x 4cm (6 x 1½in) of E for the loop

Additional requirements:
- 2 pieces of lightweight fusible volume fleece batting 16.5 x 21.5cm (6½ x 8½in)
- 21.5 x 21.5cm (8½ x 8½in) of lightweight interfacing for the large compartment
- 12.5 x 21.5cm (5 x 8½in) of lightweight interfacing for the mobile compartment
- 7.5 x 22.5cm (3 x 9in) of lightweight interfacing for the pen compartment
- 15 x 4cm (6 x 1½in) of lightweight interfacing for the hanging loop

Handbag Organiser

Size: 18 x 13 x 3cm (7 x 5 x 1¼in)

Sewing

1 Iron the two pieces of volume fleece batting on to the back of the two outside pieces (A and D). Iron all the pieces of lightweight interfacing on to the corresponding pieces of printed cotton fabric.

2 For the large compartment, fold the fabric (B) in half lengthways, right sides facing and sew around all sides, leaving a turning hole. Turn the right way out, then iron and sew up the turning hole by hand. Now position the piece on to the right side of the back piece. Edgestitch to secure the compartment to the back using a zigzag stitch along the bottom and both side edges. Be sure to leave the top open for use as a pocket.

3 For the pen compartment, fold the fabric (C) in half widthways, right sides facing, and sew around all sides, leaving a turning hole. Turn the right way out, then iron and sew up the turning hole by hand. Place on to the right side of the front piece and position it 3.5cm (1½in) from the top edge and 2.5cm (1in) from the left-hand side edge. Edgestitch the sides and bottom edge then sew once vertically down the centre to divide the pocket.

4 For the mobile pocket, fold the piece of fabric (B) in half widthways, right sides facing, and sew around all sides, leaving a turning hole. Turn the right way out, then iron and sew up the turning hole by hand. Fold the side edges of the piece 2cm (¾in) in and iron. Then fold these side flaps again 1cm (½in) back toward the side edge (like an accordion) and iron flat. Place the mobile pocket on the front piece next to the pen compartment 2cm (¾in) from the top edge and 2.5cm (1in) from the right-hand side edge. Edgestitch the side edges, then the bottom edges, pressing the pleats flat.

5 Make the strap as described on page 11. Make a loop and position it so it lies horizontally 2cm (¾in) below the top edge of the front piece with two pockets attached. The looped end should be facing toward the middle of the piece overlapping the pockets.

6 Now place the back piece on top, right sides facing, and sew the sides and bottom edges together, securing the fabric loop in the seam. Sew the base corners at a width of 3cm (1¼in) (see page 11) to form a box shape. Turn right sides out.

7 Sew the two lining pieces in the same way, right sides facing and leaving a turning hole.

Finishing off

Slip the outer fabric into the lining pieces, right sides facing. Sew the pieces together along the top edges. Turn the right way, then iron and sew up the turning hole by hand.

Materials

For the outside and the lining:
- ♥ 6 different scraps of printed cotton fabric each 20cm (8in) long and in different widths (4–6cm/1½–2½in)
- ♥ 20 x 25cm (8 x 10in) of printed cotton fabric

For the padding:
- ♥ 20 x 25cm (8 x 10in) of thin volume fleece batting

Additional requirements:
- ♥ 35cm (13¾in) of bias binding in a matching colour

Tissue Holder

Size: 13 x 8 x 2cm (5 x 3¼ x ¾in)

Sewing

1 Lay out the lining, wrong side up, and place the volume fleece batting on top. Sew the fabric strips on using the quilt-as-you-go technique (see page 13).

2 Trim the piece to 15 x 18cm (6 x 7in) and edge the short ends with bias binding.

3 Fold the bound edges in to the middle, right sides facing, with the trimmed edges overlapping to the width of the bias binding. Sew the top and bottom edges together; neaten the seam allowances with zigzag stitch.

Finishing off

Turn the holder right sides out and iron. Insert tissues from a pocket pack.

Tip

The bias binding shown in the photograph is made from two 4 x 15cm (1½ x 6in) strips of fabric cut diagonally (at 45°) from a square of fabric. Fold the fabric strips as explained on page 11 for making handles. Now you can attach your homemade binding.

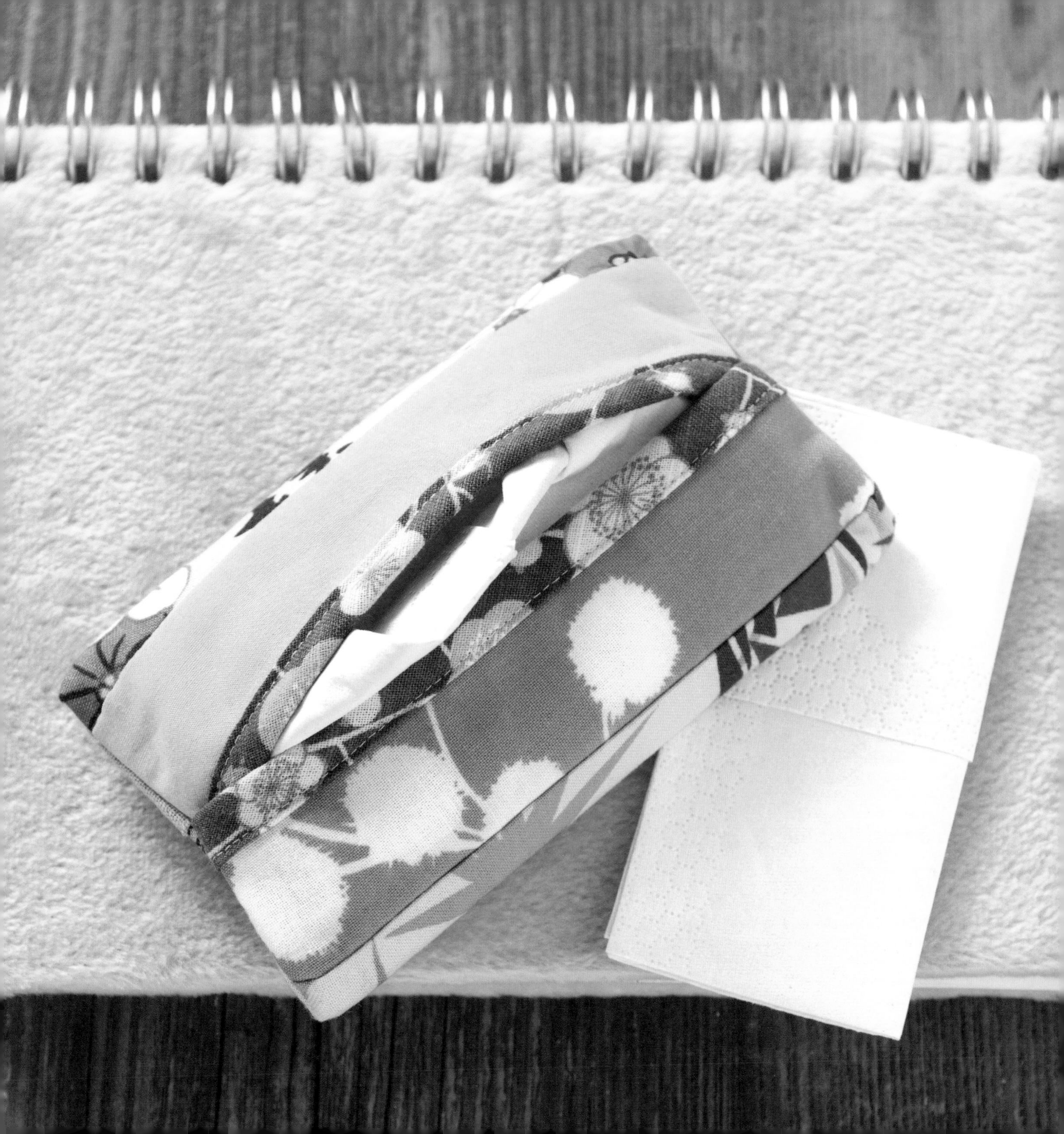

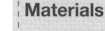

Key Purse

Size: 6 x 8cm (2½ x 3¼in)
Template: page 63

Materials

For the outside and lining:
- 4 different remnants 8 x 8cm (3¼ x 3¼in) of printed cotton fabric (outsides)
- 2 pieces 10 x 8cm (4 x 3¼in) of printed cotton fabric (lining)

For the padding:
- 10 x 20cm (4 x 8in) of volume fleece batting

Additional requirements:
- 1 zip, 10cm (4in), in a matching colour
- Bias binding, 50cm (20in), in a matching colour

Cutting out

When cutting to the template do not add a seam allowance, but add 0.75cm (¼in) to the middle seam when cutting out the four fabric pieces for the outside.

- Cut four pieces of printed cotton fabric as per the template. Cut two pieces then invert the fabric to cut two more corresponding pieces; you will end up with two mirrored pairs of different fabrics. Add a 0.75cm (¼in) seam allowance along the middle seam for the outside
- Cut two pieces of printed cotton fabric. Double the size of the template before cutting the two pieces. The fabric fold on the template is labelled to indicate the central fold for the lining
- Cut two pieces of volume fleece using the template in the same way as for the lining

Sewing

1 Sew two pieces of the smaller printed cotton fabric (those not cut on the fold) together along their central seam. Iron the seam open then attach one of the pieces of volume fleece batting as backing. Repeat this process for the remaining two pieces of printed cotton fabric for the outsides.

2 Place one fleece-backed outside piece of fabric against one lining piece, wrong sides facing, and sew all round with a zigzag stitch. Sew bias binding along the straight top outside edge but leave unsecured on the lining side. Repeat this process for the remaining outside and lining pieces.

3 Place the zip, right side up, on the lining side of one of these pieces. Position the edge of the zip parallel to the top edge and sew the zip edge between the bias binding and the lining fabric, securing the zip edge in place. Sew the opposite edge of the zip into the same position on the other fabric piece.

4 Position the two sides of the purse together, wrong sides facing, and sew the outer edges in a zigzag stitch.

Finishing off

Sew bias binding to the outside edge, leaving a 10cm (4in) excess on one corner. Fold the overlap and edgestitch in a loop. Fold the remainder of the bias binding to the other side and secure by hand stitching.

Materials

For the outside and lining:
- ♥ 90 x 20cm (43 x 8in) of printed cotton fabric

For the padding:
- ♥ 20 x 15cm (8 x 6in) of thin iron-on volume fleece batting

Additional requirements:
- ♥ 1 zip, 10cm (4in), in a matching colour
- ♥ Bias binding, 40cm (16in), in a matching colour

Cutting out

Do not include seam allowances.
- ♥ Cut four pieces of printed cotton fabric using the template
- ♥ Cut three pieces of volume fleece batting using the template

Coin Purse

Size: 12cm (4¾in)
Template: page 63

Sewing

1 For the outside, iron volume fleece batting on to the wrong side of three circles of the printed cotton fabric. Fold two pieces in half with the wrong sides facing and iron.

2 Push the zip tab under the fold of one of the folded pieces and edgestitch using the zip foot of your sewing machine. Sew the other folded pieces on to the other side of the zip in the same way.

3 Position the unfolded, fleece-backed piece of printed cotton fabric right side down, then place the fourth piece on top of it with the wrong sides facing. Then place the front, fabric piece (with the zip) on top; the right side should be facing up. Stitch around the edges of the whole piece in a zigzag stitch.

Finishing off

Sew bias binding all round the purse using a topstitch.

Shoulder Bag

Size: 22 x 30cm (8¾ x 12in) (plus handles)
Templates A and B: page 63

Materials

For the outside and lining:
- 140 x 50cm (43 x 20in) of red and white spotted cotton fabric
- 10 different-sized fabric scraps for the appliqué

For the padding:
- 50 x 60cm (20 x 24in) of thin fusible volume fleece batting

Additional requirements:
- 1 round magnetic catch
- 80cm (31½in) of imitation leather strap, 2.5cm (1in) wide
- 1 remnant of medium-firm iron-on interfacing

Cutting out

When cutting out to templates, add 0.75cm (¼in) seam allowance on all sides.
- Cut four pieces of red and white spotted cotton fabric using template A (outsides, lining)
- Cut one piece of red and white spotted cotton fabric using template B (outside pocket)
- Cut two pieces of volume fleece batting using template A for the outsides
- Cut one piece of volume fleece batting 16 x 27cm (6½ x 10½in) for the patchwork

Sewing

1 For the outside pocket, arrange the fabric remnants on the 16 x 27cm (6½ x 10½in) volume fleece batting and, using straight stitches, sew the pieces on using the patchwork technique (see page 12).

2 Sew parallel vertical lines 1cm (½in) apart over the top of the piece. Trim the completed patchwork pieces using template B (adding a seam allowance on all sides).

3 Position the spotted cotton fabric piece on top of the trimmed patchwork piece, right sides facing, and stitch all round the edges leaving a turning hole. Trim back the seam allowances. Turn the pocket right sides out and iron. Close the turning hole by hand.

4 For the outsides, iron volume fleece batting on to the backs of two pieces of red and white spotted cotton fabric cut from template A. Place the outside pocket, right side up, on the right side of one of these outside pieces and edgestitch along the rounded edge.

5 Iron a piece of interfacing measuring approximately 3 x 3cm (1¼ x 1¼in) on to the middle of the wrong side of each of the two lining pieces approximately 3cm (1¼in) below the top edges. These provide reinforcement for the magnetic catches.

6 Place the outside pieces of the bag together with the right sides facing and sew the rounded edge together. Do the same with the lining pieces, but leave a turning hole.

7 Attach the magnetic catch to the middle of the right sides of the lining and approximately 3cm (1¼in) below the top edges, making sure that the two pieces are exactly facing each other.

8 Position the ends of the carrying strap, right sides facing, at the tops of the side seams of the outer fabric and sew them into place securely. Slip the lining over the outside pieces, making sure the seams and outer edges fit together neatly. Sew the top edges together, securing the carrying strap in the seam.

Finishing off

Turn the bag right sides out through the hole in the lining and iron neatly. Close the turning hole with hand stitches.

Templates

Bottle Bag
Pages 24–25
(Base)
No seam allowance

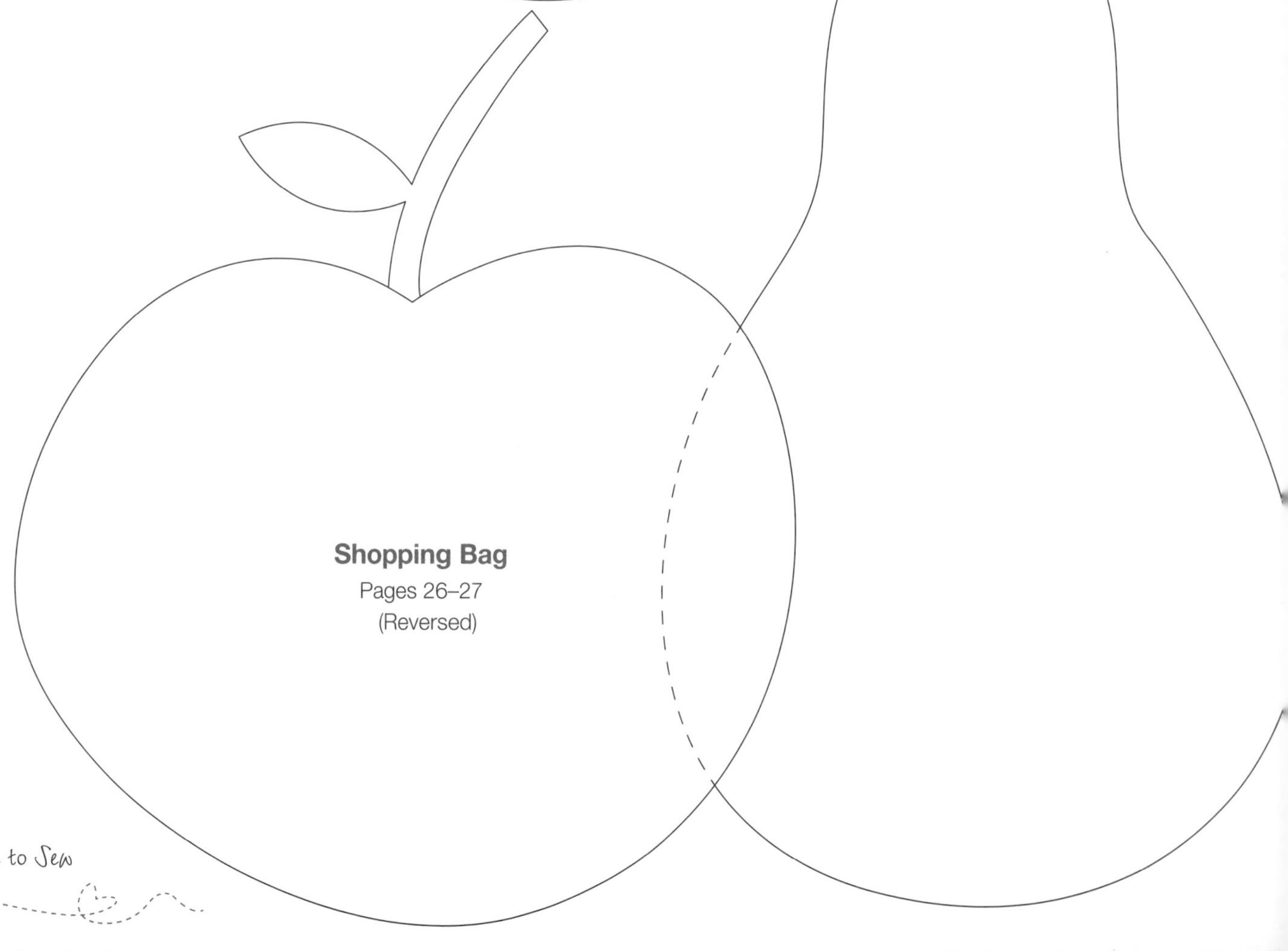

Shopping Bag
Pages 26–27
(Reversed)

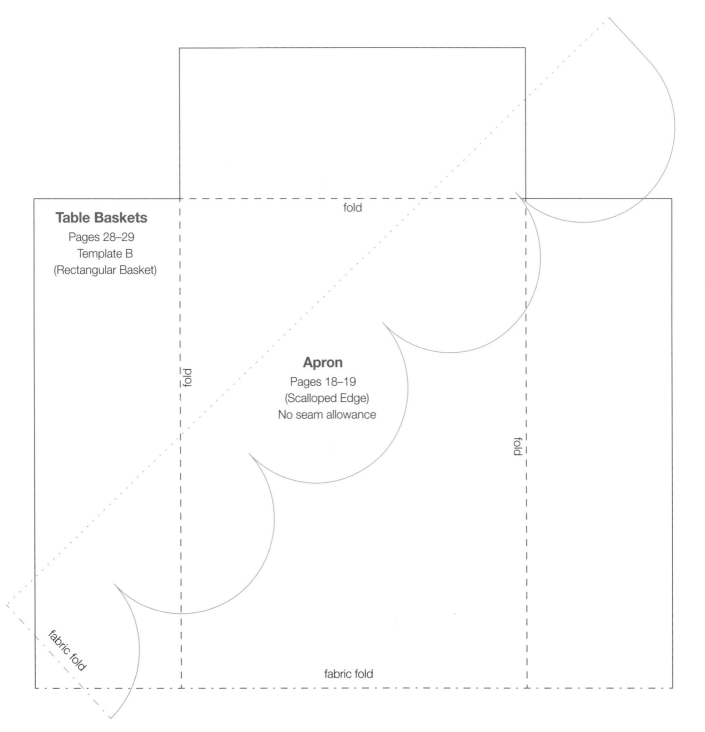

Table Baskets

Pages 28–29
Template B
(Rectangular Basket)

Apron

Pages 18–19
(Scalloped Edge)
No seam allowance

fold

fold

fold

fabric fold

fabric fold

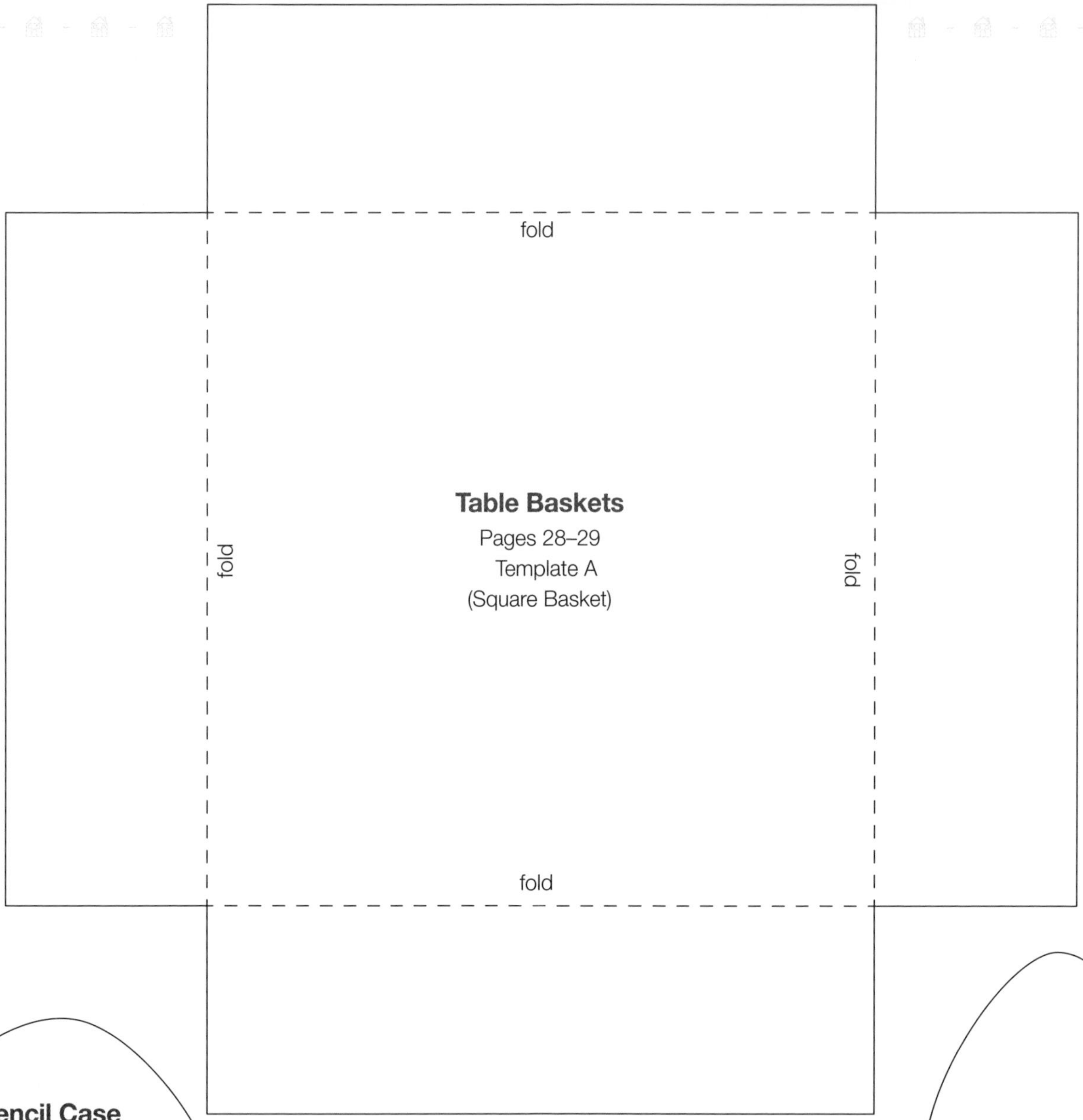

fold

fold

fold

Table Baskets

Pages 28–29

Template A

(Square Basket)

fold

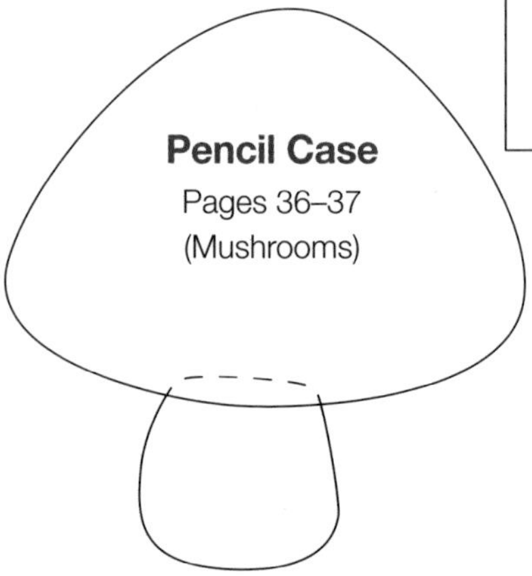

Pencil Case

Pages 36–37

(Mushrooms)

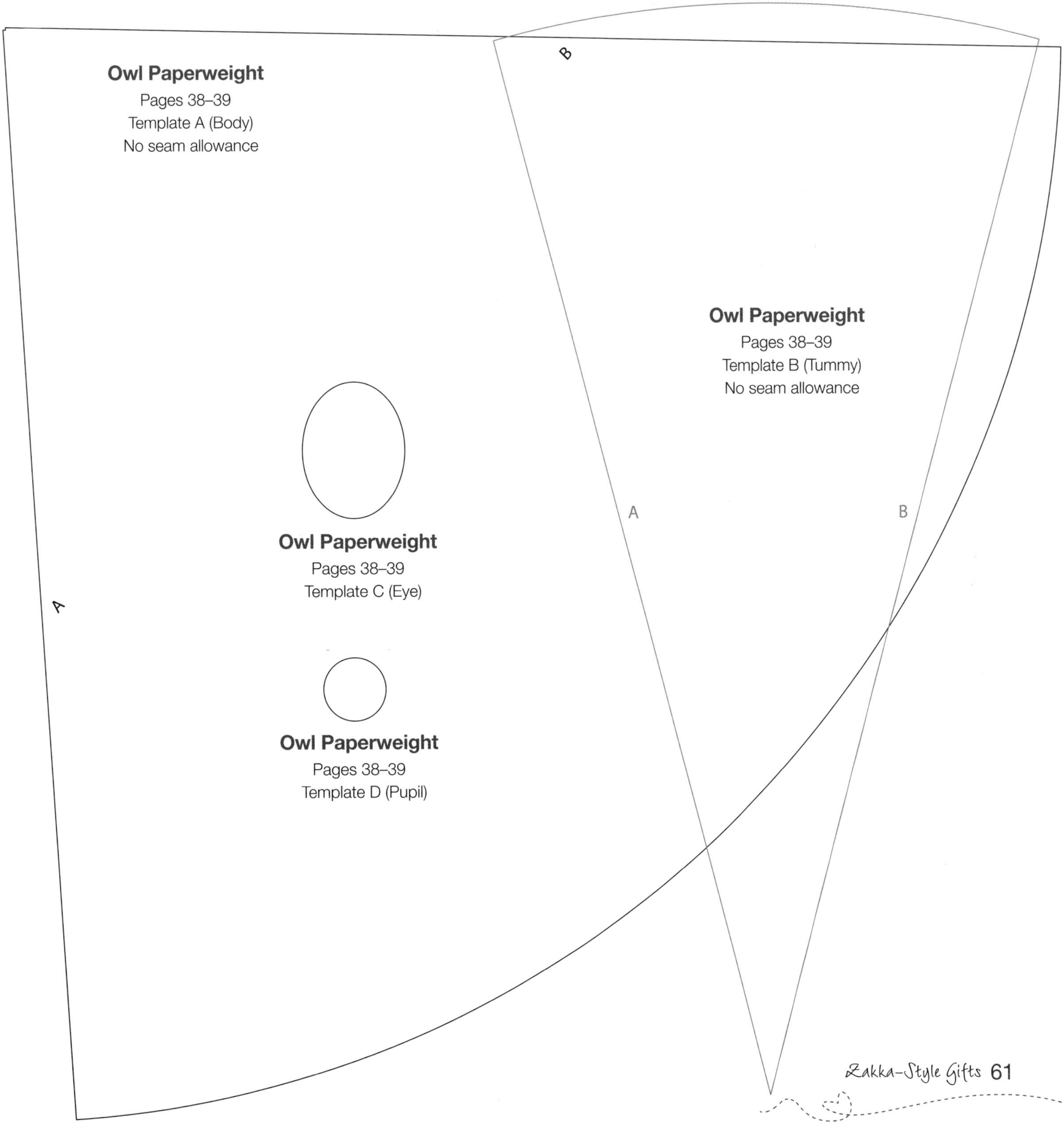

Owl Paperweight

Pages 38–39

Template A (Body)

No seam allowance

B

Owl Paperweight

Pages 38–39

Template B (Tummy)

No seam allowance

A

B

Owl Paperweight

Pages 38–39

Template C (Eye)

Owl Paperweight

Pages 38–39

Template D (Pupil)

A

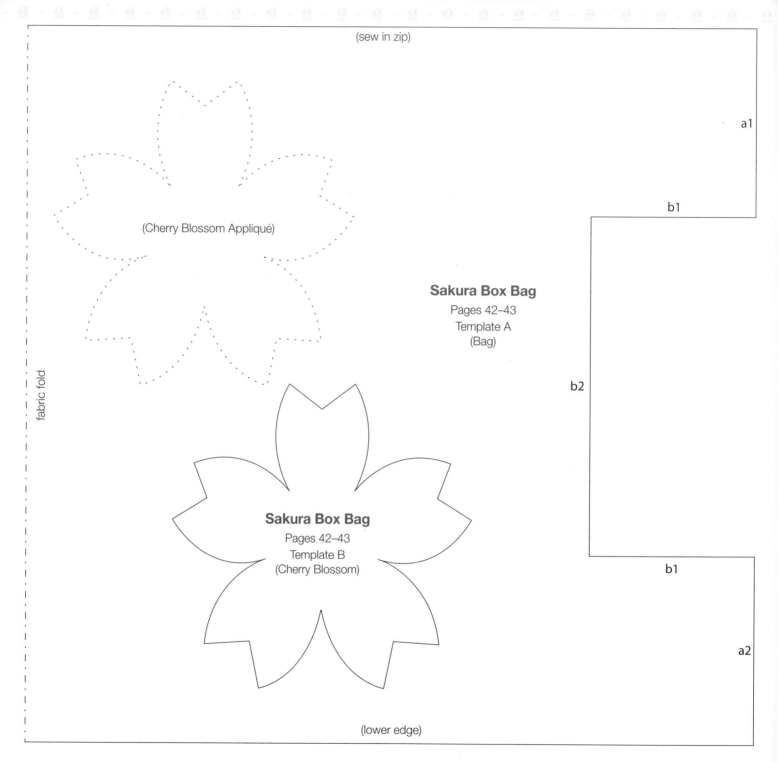

(sew in zip)

a1

b1

fabric fold

(Cherry Blossom Appliqué)

Sakura Box Bag

Pages 42–43

Template A

(Bag)

b2

b1

Sakura Box Bag

Pages 42–43

Template B

(Cherry Blossom)

a2

(lower edge)

Coin Purse

Pages 54–55

No seam allowance

Camera Bag

Pages 46–47

No seam allowance

fabric fold

**Mirror template
at fold**

**Double template
at fold**

fabric fold

Shoulder Bag

Pages 56–57

Template B (Outside Pocket)

No seam allowance

Shoulder Bag

Pages 56–57

Template A (Outside)

No seam allowance

Enlarge to 200%

Key Purse

Pages 52–53

fabric fold

**Mirror template
at fold**